"Just Common Sense"

"Just Common Sense" *Leadership Lessons*
Danny Williams
Copyright 2006

All rights reserved.

Printed and bound in the United States of America. Except as permitted under the U.S. Copyright Act of 1976, no part of this may be reproduced or distributed in any form or stored in a database or retrieval system without prior written permission from the publisher
or author.

ISBN# 978-0-9791154-1-7 0-9791154-1-8
First Edition - Second Printing October 2012

Library of Congress number pending

Published by Main Street Publishing Inc., Jackson, Tennessee.
Printed and bound by Net Pub Corporation, Poughkeepsie, New York

Written by Danny Williams
Cover design by Annette W. Galloway and Danny Williams
Cover photograph used with permission by Steve Jackson and Ty Dyer
Copy Editing by Annette W. Galloway
Editing by Pat Little

For information write to Main Street Publishing, Inc., 206 East Main Street, Suite 207, P.O. Box 696, Jackson, TN. 38302.
Toll-free 1-866-457-7379.

E-mail Danny Williams at dcwstory@yahoo.com.
Visit us at www.mainstreetpublishing.com or www.mspbooks.com

"Just Common Sense"

Leadership Lessons

By Danny Williams

Main Street Publishing, Inc. Jackson, Tn 38301

"Just Common Sense"

"Danny Williams has written a book that reminds that we don't have to make life or work as complicated as we often try to. The theme of common sense lessons are woven throughout Danny's personal stories- and the stories are a pleasure to read. This book will make you feel better about yourself and your work. I recommend it!

Joe Calloway

"Just Common Sense"

Table of Contents

Introduction 13

Chapter One - DAD 17

Chapter Two - THE RAKE 19

Chapter Three - SOAP BOX DERBY 24

Chapter Four - THE RABBIT HUNT 30

Chapter Five - THE SQUIRREL HUNT 34

Chapter Six - MALICIOUS MISCHIEF 41

Chapter Seven - GOOD MISS 46

Chapter Eight - TRAFFIC 52

Chapter Nine - THE MAN 57

Chapter Ten - FLY FISHING 62

Chapter Eleven - THE SPARE TIRE 68

"Just Common Sense"

Acknowledgements

    These stories have been in my head and on my heart for many years. They have been easy to tell but at times have been difficult to put on paper. Many people have put up with me during this process, and I think they ought to know I appreciate them.

    To the folks at Main Street Publishing, this would never have been possible without you. Annette, thanks for your patience and input. Pat thanks for making me sound so good.

    To the teams of great people I've had the good fortune to lead, I hope I encouraged you enough, was human enough, and dealt with each of you justly enough. You deserved my best.

    To my buddies Mike, Ricky, Ed, and Mark, you all looked at me funny when I said I was doing this. Don't worry; the names have been changed to protect the innocent. Each of you shared these stories with me; each of you blessed my life.

    To my girls Sarah-Gray and Ann-Alece, you have made it possible for me to understand unconditional love. I could not be prouder of you both and could not have dreamed a better dream than of being your daddy.

    To my wife; Debbie, you are the person I most desire to be like. Your positive attitude, the way you love us, and your faith in God and me is humbling. The best thing about me is you.

"Just Common Sense"

Danny Williams

Dedication

In the book <u>The Prophet,</u> written in 1923 by Kahlil Gibran, the author writes in the chapter on teaching: "If he (the teacher) is indeed wise he does not bid you enter the house of his wisdom, but rather leads you to the threshold of your own mind."

I have been passionate in my pursuit for knowledge regarding the art of management and leadership. In my quest, nothing or no one I studied provided as much insight into leadership as a common man of meager education and modest means. I've attempted every technique that I was taught or observed, and not one had the impact on me like the common sense approach of my dad. This book is dedicated to him and to his lessons that did not attempt to lead me into the house of his wisdom but opened my mind to the wisdom that was within me.

Thanks, Dad. I wish we had had time to make some new stories together. I would have tried harder.

"Just Common Sense"

Introduction

    I never met him, but I knew as much about him as any close family member. Dad spoke of Papa in the most reverent of tones and often told me that, if not for Papa, he would never have survived the war.

    Dad shipped out for New Guinea in April of 1942, just one month after he and momma married. He left his young bride, his family, and his home to enter into the most hostile environment he had ever known. His stories of malaria, dysentery, monsoon rains, and dense jungle reminded me of the Tarzan movies we watched together almost every Saturday morning.

    Dad's combat unit was stationed near the north shore with its large, impassable mangrove swamps that made movement of large formations impossible. It was here that Dad met Papa, a Papuan from a tiny coastal settlement. Papa's ancestors had crossed the land bridge, long since covered by ocean, from Australia thousands of years before, but Papa still resembled the traditional aboriginal Bushmen that had occupied this paradise for centuries. Papa had hunted and explored every inch of this, the second largest island in the world and he knew it like the back of his hand. He knew all the small dirt trails, barely a yard wide, that led through the lush rain forest and every pass in the mountains that split the middle of the island. He knew how to find shelter from the downpours that occurred daily and how to get across swollen rivers safely. Papa taught Dad to use native secrets so that he would not fall victim to malaria or dengue fever. Most importantly, Papa taught Dad how to use the dense vegetation for concealment from the enemy during their

"Just Common Sense"

frequent supply missions.

Many times during the hot, humid days and the frightening, lonely nights, Papa's presence and knowledge assured Dad that he would one day return to the safety of home. Papa had been hired to be a guide for the troops in Dad's unit. "Without Papa," Dad said, "the jungle would have swallowed us up."

Because of his faithful guide Dad was able to return home safely to his family and friends. Dad began his business career with a determination to give his family all the things he had sacrificed while he was growing up. Most importantly to him, he wanted me to have a college education, something no one in my family had the opportunity to acquire before.

It's been almost thirty years since I finished my college experience, and what an experience it was. I attempted varsity athletics only to find that there is nothing like a good little man except a good big one. I struggled with courses I wasn't prepared for and struggled with managing my time wisely. I spent enough time at college bars to get a degree, and I rode a bicycle to raise money for the Baptist Student Union. My college life was often a contradiction and an exploration. College was a thrill ride and I enjoyed every minute of it. I especially enjoyed my major course of study. I went to college to become a game warden, so I could live my life in the woods that I loved so well. A mentor of mine was the local game warden in my hometown, and he encouraged me to go into the wildlife field; and with my love for the outdoors, I thought I had found my calling, until about a week before graduation.

While in college, I had met and married the love of my life. Dad had approved of my decision, but not my timing. He had encouraged us to wait, but love won out. Now with graduation looming on our horizon, I realized spending all my time in the woods might spoil my enjoyment of what had always been my hobbies. Since I didn't play golf, what was I going to do with my free time? I admire those guys and gals that pursued the wildlife field. They work long hours for not enough pay and often put themselves in harm's way to protect the environment and its resources. After an interview for a job as park ranger, I returned home to my young wife full of doubt about my plans for our future. It was a fine time to discover I had invested so much in my education only to find that pursuing a career in the wildlife field may turn out to be a terrible mistake for me.

A friend had taken a job in sales and was convinced he was going to make his fortune. He convinced me as well, and I began down a path I have never regretted. It turns out I was good at it. Sales required two things I had an abundance of since birth: confidence and the ability to talk. Through the years there have been moments of dizzying brilliance and moments of utter defeat that have been a roller coaster ride of exhilaration and dread. Through it all, I have pursued the mastery of the craft of sales, particularly the management and leadership of others.

Like everyone else in the business world, I have attended seminars, workshops, and training sessions on everything from talking on the telephone to negotiating multi-million dollar deals. I even spent three days in a crowded conference room with about fifty others learning how to use one of those fancy, leather-bound organizers that I gave to my kids when I got home. I believe you die a slow death in sales if you aren't organized, but the method one person uses may not work for everyone. "Just common sense," Dad would say.

My life on the stormy sea of corporate do's and don'ts is what prompted the writing of this book. I never really found anyone that unselfishly committed himself to my success. Personal agendas and aspirations always

"Just Common Sense"

overshadowed the feelings and contributions of others. I often felt "swallowed up" as Dad had said about the jungle of New Guinea because I lacked a competent guide to see me through the dense undergrowth of the business world. I discovered experience at leading does not always equal competency at leading, and tyranny does not ever equal lasting results. Where people are valued there is no place for intimidation and threats, which are often used by weak leaders. In all the training sessions, in all the workshops, watching and observing all the so- called masters in the art of managing and leadership, I had none that could compare to the simple common sense approach my dad took to guiding me.

The stories that follow are but a few of the many lessons I learned about real leadership when I didn't even realize it. Like Papa did for him in the jungles of New Guinea, my dad's lessons have guided me through many perilous situations and helped me and others find the safety and security we sought on the steep mountain slopes of corporate America.

You, my reader, have made an investment, and I feel responsible to give you the best advice I can about leadership and management. I'll tell you what Dad would say, "Do unto others as you would have them do unto you; that's just common sense."

Chapter One

DAD

"……Help me, Danny"

He was a big man in his prime that was well over six foot tall and pushing 230 pounds. Now lying on his hospital bed, he looked so small and frail. Hair that I had never seen out of place was bushy and tattered. A scraggly beard had grown on a face that was blotchy and red. His arms had once held me up to touch the moon; now they were restrained to keep him from pulling out the feeding tube in his nose. His last words to me were, "Help me, Danny."

I wanted to help more than he could know or understand. I wanted to set him free. This was no way for a man like my Dad to spend the last moments of his life. I wanted to put him in my car and drive. We'd roll the windows down, listen to Patsy Cline or Nat King Cole on his eight track tape player, and head to the shore of Mississippi or Las Vegas, two of his favorite places in the world. Watch out mommas; the Williams' boys were on the loose…better lock up your daughters. I wanted to live dangerously, drive fast, and be free, but he couldn't, not anymore. He was too weak and he was dying.

I had looked up to him all my life. Now, I was standing beside him looking down at a man I barely recognized. He had cast a formidable figure; now he was no longer intimidating.

My Dad and I had struggled with our relationship for most of our lives. I had rebelled, grown my hair long, and

"Just Common Sense"

wanted to go my own way. However, he had never let go of his dreams for me. I had run as fast as I could in the opposite direction. I had run away from home, told him that I hated him once, and tried everything he hoped that I would not. Now, standing at his side, his words, his approval, his lessons about life were the most important thing in my world. I wanted to listen to his words. I wanted to please him. I wanted the instruction he was so willing to give. Now was too late.

In the last few moments of his life, Dad spoke of Papa as if he were looking for his trusted friend and guide to lead him into the unfamiliar territory he was about to enter. The baby boy of Launa and Joe Williams died on June 30, 2002. His wife, my mom, died 26 years earlier. He had grieved and missed her each moment of each passing year. Now they were together once again. I was an only child, adopted into this man's world when I was two years old. During my growing-up years, I regretted, at times, my being adopted. Now I regret we didn't have more time.

I learned many lessons when Dad thought I wasn't paying attention. He would never know what an impact he had been on my life. My pride and ego never really allowed me to tell him all the things I learned by watching and listening in the background. I could not have realized during all those years that his common sense approach to things and his sound judgment would impact me so much as I entered the world of business.

Chapter Two
THE RAKE
"...a businessman needs the proper tools in order to be successful"

Like most boys raised in the southern deciduous hardwood region of the country, I raked leaves in the fall to make spending money. I'd make a few dollars to buy BB's, fishing lures, and cotton candy (when the fair came to town). Hardwood trees, I discovered at an early age, do not hold onto their leaves in the fall. Most folks in the South, especially little old ladies, liked to see the dead brown Bermuda grass on their yards and not the clutter of dead leaves. They would give an industrious young man a dollar or two if he raked the leaves in neat piles, kept the other kids from jumping in the piles, and sacked the leaves in huge black plastic bags. The bags of leaves would be placed out by the curb and the City would come by in a big truck and pick them up. I never knew what the City did with all those bags of leaves, or why they wanted them. The best my 10-year-old mind could figure was that our town needed more dirt. It's a scientific fact that if you let leaves lie around long enough, they will eventually turn to dirt, unlike those huge black plastic bags that will never rot. I figured our City must need all those leaves to produce dirt for some secret government project. I wasn't sure, but I did know that I did not get paid until they were bagged and out by the curb. I decided I was just happy to help the City with their dirt-producing project if that got me paid.

Leaf raking was not an easy or pleasant job. Many times

"Just Common Sense"

I wished that we would move out to Arizona with my aunt. If the pictures she sent were any indication, they didn't have leaves in Arizona. They probably didn't have any grumpy old ladies either that were never completely pleased with the job you did and never wanted to pay the full agreed-upon price. So many times, moving to Arizona looked like the best option to me. Having decided that I needed money for all the important things in life and that putting up with little old ladies would help me get it, I set out each afternoon to the tool shed to get the tool of my chosen profession…The Rake.

The Rake…it was an eight-foot, wooden-handled, metal-toothed, heavy as an anvil, scepter from hell itself, designed to wear out a 10-year-old boy in only minutes of use. No doubt it had been invented by the same guy that invented that dunking machine made so famous during the Salem witch trials that I had read about in school. That contraption forced confessions of all sorts of wrongdoing out of otherwise good folks, and my rake was just such a tool. Each afternoon as I stood in front of that tool shed, Arizona looked like what I pictured heaven to look like from my momma's descriptions.

My momma…she loved her baby boy and spoiled him rotten, everyone said. I never really understood that comment until much later in life. My momma was so proud that I was working so hard to make my own money. My momma also knew that I would quit soon if I had to continue to use that old rake. On one crisp fall afternoon as I was walking out the door to head to the shed, momma stopped me in my tracks. She looked directly at my dad, who was reading the afternoon newspaper and did the unthinkable. She interrupted him. Reading the newspaper before the evening news broadcast came on was a ritual for my dad. It was like cleaning his gun after a hunting trip or a prayer of thanks before each meal. It was a sacred time when he did not want to be disturbed. It was vital, in Dad's opinion, to keep up with current events. How else would it be possible to complain at every opportunity about politicians, taxes, or the growing epidemic of welfare in the country. "Daddy," she said. Momma always called him Daddy for reasons I also never understood until much later. "Daddy, this boy can't use that old rake any longer. He's too small for it. He can't get his work done efficiently, and you need to get up and go buy him one that he can use."

All I could think was what had she done. I started running in one place as if I were throwing a rock and seeing it in slow motion go straight for the neighbor's window. You know disaster is on the way, and there is suddenly the urge to get out of there mixed with the fear to move. I was too afraid to stand still and too afraid not to because he was going to think I had put her up to this. Why had she bothered him during his paper reading ritual, why had God made leaves in the first place, and how long would it take me to walk to Arizona. I prepared for the hounds of hell to be unleashed and saw what had been a brief life pass before my eyes. The evening paper slid slowly down. Dad folded it neatly, placed it on the coffee table and rose to his feet. He was a big man sitting down, but standing, he looked like a giant. Here it comes, I thought, and braced myself.

With eyes squeezed shut, I heard him say, "Honey, you're right; a businessman needs the proper tools if he is going to be successful."

I almost passed out from holding my breath, and it took Momma several minutes to fully revive me, so I could walk without falling down.

Dad and I drove in silence that afternoon to the place where all tools were purchased in 1964. For that matter, most everything of value to a 10-year- old boy or a 40-year-old man came from the same place, the Western Auto store. It

"Just Common Sense"

was a familiar place filled with distinct sounds and smells. The store was filled with customers and friendly store clerks that could find even the most uncommon bolt or nut for even those foreign-made tools. Dad knew everyone, and he called them by name, asking about wives and children that were away at college. Families and jobs were discussed, and a game of checkers refused as he smiled and told them about his young, enterprising boy and his need of the proper tools. Approving nods and winks came my way, and I felt like one of the boys as we made our way to the garden section.

On the back wall there must have been 200 different shapes, sizes, handle types, and name brands of rakes that were all made in America in 1964. This leaf-raking business must be big, I thought, and I'm going to make my fortune in no time. I raced to the first one I could grab and pretended to be using it when Dad let out a little chuckle. "Hold on there, son; we've got as long as it takes. Let's find the one that is just right for you."

We spent the rest of the afternoon and into the evening trying out almost every rake in the store. A few times the guys would get up and check on us to make sure we were finding everything okay. Dad pointed out the benefits and shortcomings of each one. He talked about quality and workmanship and brand names with long histories of customer satisfaction. Dad knew that just any rake would not do and that taking the time and having the patience to pick out the one that was a perfect fit for my small hands would allow me to work without tiring. The tool that had the perfect fit would increase my chances for success and teach me the joy of working. If I succeeded or if I did not, it wouldn't be because he hadn't given me every chance he could.

Danny Williams

I learned a lot that day about rakes. I learned about the time that is necessary to teach others how to find the tool that works best for them and the proper use of it. I learned that it takes caring about others' success and putting your comfort second as my dad had done for me. On the way home that evening with my new rake riding in the backseat, I said, "Thanks, Dad, for my new rake."

He said, "Your welcome, Son. It's just common sense. A businessman has to have the proper tools to be successful. Everyone is different, and that's why they make so many different kinds. All I did was help you pick out the best one for you and give you some tips I've picked up from experience. Now, son, it's up to you to make the most of it."

Chapter Three
SOAP BOX DERBY
"...it's about being in the race"

In 1965 at the age of 11, I could think of few things that compared to participating in one of this country's greatest events, the Soap Box Derby. I am sure this race between boys in a homemade soapbox car spawned many participants in the now crazy world of NASCAR. The local events around the country brought boys and their dads out in mass in the hopes of winning an opportunity to race in the national finals held in Akron, Ohio. The details of how the whole thing first hooked me are unclear. However, I remember Dad's childlike enthusiasm for the event and the competition as if it were yesterday.

We attended rallies at the local movie theater on Saturday afternoons and watched films of previous soapbox derbies from around the country. There were specific rules about cars that were to be built by the participants and certain components were supplied, such as wheels, steering wheels, and those really cool crash helmets. Everyone was given ideas about building racers, but in the end it was your own design and materials, as long as they were within the guidelines established by the national office.

Dad and I never missed a meeting. We watched every film and discussed exactly how we would build an aerodynamic soapbox missile that I would ride to victory. We collected all the supplied materials and set off for home with plans of standing in the winner's circle and going to

Akron. I didn't know where Akron was or, for that matter, where Ohio was, but I was ready to go.

Dad's buddy at the Western Auto Store was happy to see us when we arrived with our list of materials needed to build my racer. Usually a trip to Western Auto would have been a half-day ritual, but not this time. We were on a mission. Dad purchased plywood for the floor and cross braces. We needed 2 x 4's, miscellaneous screws, nails, L brackets, and cables. We bought saws, hammers, levels, and things I am sure we never used. We were like sharks on a feeding frenzy. Once we tasted blood, we tore through the store in a fever pitch, devouring everything in sight. I am not sure what the total bill came to when we checked out, but I remember Dad saying, "Are you sure?" He paid and we were in business.

We followed the rules regarding building my derby racer by the letter. They were there for a reason, Dad said, so we would stick to them — no questions asked. We measured and made templates for the floor. We assembled the braking device as discussed during one of our many rally meetings. The ribs were cut and fastened to the floor with screws and L brackets. The axles and wheels that were officially sanctioned and supplied were secured, and the steering wheel mechanism was installed to give me total control over the rocket ship I would eventually captain to my dreams. We chose a lightweight design and material for our exterior covering. We spent many hours of toiling side by side after dad got home from work in the afternoons and on into the evenings. My dream rocket ship was ready.

All we could do was stand back and admire our craftsmanship. Dad beamed with pride at our effort and showed everyone in the neighborhood our masterpiece. Momma was dragged outside away from her household

"Just Common Sense"

duties to add her special blend of encouragement and caution. "Make sure you have on clean underwear when you race," she said, "If you have a wreck and have to go to the hospital, you need to have on clean underwear." Momma was big on that idea about my underwear.(She was also adamant about my always having money to call home. I had a dime taped inside every pair of shoes I owned until I was 19 years old, so I could call home if I got in trouble and needed help.)

We were ready. Our soapbox derby racer had been only an idea just a few weeks earlier. Now it was a reality. Colonial Bakery was my sponsor, and they printed their name on both sides of my car. Dad and I spent many Saturday mornings eating fresh baked bread we purchased from Colonial Bakery just when it came out of the ovens. We would go downtown to the factory with a stick of butter for each of us in tow. We would purchase two piping hot loaves of bread, cut them in half, and place a whole stick of butter in each of them. By the time we walked across the street to the artesian well, the butter would be running down the sides of the loaves. I was happy Colonial was my sponsor. I thought that if I won, who knows, maybe some free bread. It was as good a thought as they were memories.

The day of the race arrived. The ramps where the cars would begin the downhill pursuit were at the top of Tigrett Hill. Participants would race in two's in a single elimination format. If you lost, you had to watch from the cheering crowds of moms, dads, aunts, uncles, cousins, and just regular fans of kids that were doing something to keep them out of trouble on a Saturday morning.

Losing had never crossed my mind, at least not while we were attending the pep rallies, or while we were purchasing all those materials, or while working beside Dad in the garage that was converted to a high tech race car assembly plant. Losing was never thought of during all those practice runs and certainly not in my mind's eye as I saw myself winning in my hometown and then in Akron, Ohio, against all the boys from other towns around the country. But now, just before it was my turn to fulfill my dream, all I could think about was losing. The competition looked fierce. There were cars of every shape and material type imaginable, all within the guidelines, of course. Each car had undergone a rigorous examination and checked from nose to tail the night before by the officials. Some cars were painted with flames and fire-breathing dragons. There was every color under the rainbow. There were slogans on cars that read *"I'm Fast"* and *"Greased Lightning."* Suddenly, I was petrified by the competition.

I never met anyone that thrived more on competition than my dad. I had been in every pool hall in the southern half of the United States and even parts above the Mason Dixon Line with Dad. His question to the management when we arrived would always be the same. "Who's the best shooter you got?" Every pool hall's got one. It's always the guy that all the locals brag about to the wandering wannabes. That's the guy Dad was looking for. Usually, they had their own custom-made cue stick in a leather carrying case. Dad always used a house stick. He said, "When you use a house stick, you make the competition overconfident because most guys think if you don't have your own special equipment, you should not be taken seriously. I witnessed Dad beat these guys using a house stick and playing one handed more times than I could count. He did not always win, but that was really okay with Dad. He would say it was not the winning that was so important. I always thought that it was not so much that Dad loved to win as it was that he hated to lose. To Dad it was the competition. He loved being in the fight, and he wanted to compete against the best.

Dad sensed my fear and concern as we sized up the driver and car that would be my opponent. He asked about

"Just Common Sense"

my car. "Did it handle well in the test run?"

"Yes," I replied.

"Well, then you know you can be confident about the product you have produced. Remember, a lot of care and work have been put into it. It performs as you expected, and your competition has followed the same guidelines that you did. There is no reason to believe your car is not as good as his, right?"

"No," I said.

"How about the family turnout?" he asked.

"Everyone's here," I said.

Momma had on a yellow sundress, and she never looked prettier. I had aunts, uncles, cousins, and all those other folks that were glad I was not doing something to get in trouble.

"Well, then," Dad said, "you have a good support group behind you, don't you?"

"I guess so," I managed to say.

Finally, he asked about me. "How are you?" he asked.

"I am a little nervous," I muttered, trying not to wet myself. I wondered if momma brought any clean underwear because these were in danger of not being unsoiled if I had to go to the hospital.

"A little nervous is good," Dad said. It means the blood is flowing. It's just common sense, son. You have worked hard, you have practiced, and you have seen yourself being a winner," Dad said. "It's not about crossing the finish line first. It's about being in the race. The other car looks good. When you compete against good competition, you have an opportunity to discover how good you are. Now do your best and win or lose, shake hands, and be happy you had the opportunity to compete."

It has been written that the effective job of a sales manager is that of a cheerleader. That's exactly what Dad was being that day at the top of Tigrett Hill. Dad made sure I knew that I had a product in which I could be confident. He assured me that my support system was in place and he encouraged me to put myself up against the best so that I could truly know how good I could be. Win or lose, competition is not something to fear.

I lost my race that memorable Saturday morning. The experience will always stand out in my mind as being a positive, fun adventure. Because of the common sense approach my Dad taught me that day, I may have lost the race that day, but I have won many others.

Chapter Four
THE RABBIT HUNT
"...if you want to be a good leader, you will learn to follow"

When Dad entered a room, he owned it. He was tall, handsome and spoke with unquestioning authority. His fingernails were meticulously trimmed and manicured, and his clothing would be starched, pressed, and custom tailored. His expensive Johnston & Murphy alligator shoes would be professionally shined; and, of course, his belt would match them. Only dark suits with white shirts and dark Countess Mara ties gave him the appearance of a New York lawyer. He never owned one of those pea green or sky blue leisure suits that were the trend of the day and would not have been caught dead wearing white socks. "White socks were for tennis shoes," Dad would say, and I don't think he owned a pair of those in his life. In his later years, he laughed at talk show hosts and news broadcasters that wore those same color shirt and tie combinations. If it were a pool hall or church pew, beer joint or union labor meeting, Dad would be dressed to impress, and his appearance and demeanor commanded attention. You could have never guessed that he was only able to finish the 7th grade when you witnessed his penmanship. Many marveled, as I did, at his ability to calculate large numbers in his head. Before any banker with a calculator blazing could finish entering the amount of the loan, Dad would have the monthly payment calculated. Everything about Dad let you know that he was the undeniable leader of all situations except when it came time to go rabbit hunting.

About the only thing Dad enjoyed more than taking someone's money shooting pool was rabbit hunting. His taste for Momma's barbequed rabbit rivaled his appetite for fish, and that was saying something. We spent every weekend and as many afternoons as humanly possible chasing a pack of beagle hounds in the Hatchie River bottom when the season was in.

Junior had been Dad's close friend and hunting companion for more years than Dad could remember. He had the best rabbit hounds in West Tennessee and, for that matter, possibly the best in the world, according to Dad. On the several hundred hunts I attended with Junior through my growing up years, I never heard him say much except for one memorable time when I wandered off from the group. I was making my way to a clearing in the woods to get a better shot when I heard Junior's rather harsh voice calling my name. Several colorful words preceded and followed my name that let me know I had messed up by getting out of Junior's eyesight. I heard more words in those few seconds after he found me than I had ever heard him use. Junior said that if I couldn't follow directions that I could stay home. He said there were plenty of guys who wanted to come along and that I was taking up space for those who could follow the rules. Junior said so many things in those brief moments all I could do was look down and keep my mouth shut. I thought that was the best thing for me to do, and after all these years I'm glad; for once I had enough sense to keep all the good explanations I thought of later to myself. Dad had said that Junior had been in some trouble in his past and had to go to prison for it. The rumor was that Junior had killed someone that deserved it; and I was convinced he could kill again, so I followed Dad closely after that wandering-off mistake. Junior did not care that I was Charlie's boy, and Dad allowed the lesson he was giving me to sink in before he

"Just Common Sense"

mentioned it to me.

"Junior is in charge out here, son," he said. "Don't forget it." I never did.

What I could not understand was why Dad was not in charge. He was always in charge and everyone knew it. Dad was the best shot in the group, and I never saw him miss. In all situations he was the one everyone depended on and the one whose opinion they always sought. Why did Dad allow Junior to lead him around like a puppy following a child with a popsicle? Dad always stood where Junior told him to stand and did whatever Junior told him to do. I believed that if Junior said he wanted him to walk on hot coals Dad would have started looking for branches to make the fire. Why was the question I could not hold in on the drive home from one memorable hunt.

"Cause he is the best, son, and he knows what he is doing out there," was dad's response. Look at that bunch of rabbits we are taking home today. If we had been out there by ourselves, we probably would not have had so much success as we did today. He's a good leader and a good teacher. If you want to be a good leader some day, you'll learn how to follow now. It's just common sense, son."

Dad explained to me that it took several things to make a good leader, but the most important in his opinion was safety.

"A good leader is responsible for the safety and the welfare of the group," Dad said. "Junior takes his job very seriously, as you have seen first hand. By splitting away from the group, you may have been shot in a cross fire. Junior knows that keeping everyone safe is the most important aspect of any rabbit hunt or any other activity for that matter," Dad explained. "Good leaders are protective of those that follow them. Junior was harsh with you, but he was fair and you are safe. Most importantly, you'll be around to go again tomorrow, thanks to him."

"Secondly," Dad said, "I follow Junior because he's never asked me to do anything he was not ready and willing to do himself. Good leaders can be trusted, son."

Dad went on to explain the third aspect of Junior's leadership that impressed him the most was that Junior always put everyone else's success above his own.

"Have you ever seen Junior shoot first?" Dad asked. "I haven't. He always places the rest of the group in the best place for them to be successful. He knows that by helping others succeed he also wins."

Even a twelve-year-old kid could see that Dad had the utmost respect for Junior. The leadership ability Junior had came by instinct. Dad would say, "If you want to be a good leader when it comes your turn, you'll be a good follower now." That common sense from my dad came by instinct as well.

"Just Common Sense"

Chapter Five
THE SQUIRREL HUNT
"...cling to the hope that tomorrow will be better."

It was the night before opening day of squirrel season in 1967, a night we called "squirrel eve." This night was as special to a 13-year-old boy as "duck eve" or "rabbit eve" or maybe even Christmas Eve. Dad and I had joined six other father and son teams in the old rundown logging cabin in the Hatchie River bottom that was often our home away from home. The men would sit on the front porch overlooking the river until late in the night. They would tell stories, laugh, and chew tobacco or smoke non-filter Camel cigarettes in the dim light of an oil-burning lantern. We boys would go to the windows covered with plastic sheeting that served as window panes and see the hazy red glow of their cigarettes, run back to our bunks, and tell stories of ghosts or dragons with red, glowing eyes staring in from the dark woods that surrounded us. We would laugh and wrestle on the dirty wooden floor and brag about who would come in first from the hunt the next day with the limit. The law would allow each hunter to harvest five squirrels each, and no one wanted to come in with less. Getting the limit was important to boys who were still working on the ego they thought they would need to carry them to adulthood.

Dad and I had never gone into the dark, damp forest on one of these early fall opening days and returned without reaching out goal of ten. Dad knew every inch of these woods and the best spots to assure our success. He was the best shot of the group and had taught me all his secrets while we practiced shooting cans and bottles in the off-season. He often spoke to his friends about my gift for shooting and how fortunate I had been to be born with "the eye" for it.

Sleep came difficult on these magical nights in the cabin. The eerie sounds of the night crept in from outdoors as if there were no walls surrounding us. When twelve guys bunked together for the night, they made their own blend of scary noises as well. The main contributor for the lack of sleep was the anticipation of getting into the woods before daybreak, finding that one special tree among all the others that the squirrels preferred, and bringing home the limit first. It was a competition to us boys, and I wanted to win.

Sometime during the night, I had pulled up the homemade blanket that Momma had sent for me to cover my face. Long before the sun began to rise, Dad slid it down and whispered in a low voice, "It's time." We gobbled down the donuts we brought from home, and Dad allowed me one cup of strong black coffee, usually reserved for the men. He let me drink coffee on other occasions also, but it usually had so much sugar and cream in it that it tasted more like a milkshake than coffee. Dad said I didn't need black coffee because I was strung tight enough without it; but it was opening day, and I would need to be alert and wide awake if we were going to be successful.

I watched as each father and son slowly disappeared from the warm glow of the lantern light into the dark woods around the cabin. Confidence was high, and each had scouted for the best locations days before. Dad and I walked in silence through the trees guided only by the small beam coming from his flashlight. I walked closely behind Dad; and even though I loved the forest in the early morning, the hair on the back of my neck stood straight out. I told myself that I was just excited, but in the back of my mind I wondered what may be watching us from the shadows and darkness held back just by that small flashlight. Those things do not work all the time, I thought, and how old were the batteries anyway. Had Dad remembered to change them and did Momma remember to get new ones when she went to the store to get our supplies? All these concerns raced through my mind as we slipped through the woods in silence. I walked stride for stride with Dad, and that was difficult given the length of his legs versus mine.

After several minutes of dodging branches, crossing a small creek that filled my boots with ice-cold swamp water, and tripping over an unseen log in the darkness, we arrived at our spot. Dad had picked this particular place several days before, having seen plenty of "signs" that the squirrels had been using it heavily. Tall, scaly bark hickory trees that appeared to be losing their outside covering were clumped in the middle of a huge stand of ancient oaks. These were the two types of trees Dad had always told me to find because they were the favorite choices for our quarry. We sat on the ground on folded newspapers Dad had brought in his hunting coat. Even on a hunting trip, Dad tried to remain neat and clean, a habit I never seemed to be able to acquire. Dad would say that I looked dirty getting out of the bath. I had a knack for shooting, not for staying clean. Dad took a familiar pose I had witnessed a thousand times before. His knees were bent with feet flat on the ground making it easy to rise for a good shot. His forearms rested on his knees, and the Winchester model 12 shotguns that I lusted for even as a small child cradled between his palms. Dad had paid $60.00 for that shotgun at Western Auto many years before, and it looked like it did the day he first took it from the box. His guns were always oiled and polished immediately each evening before they were safely put away. He believed in keeping his tools of every variety in the very best working order, always giving him the "best chance of success," he said.

Dad fixed his eyes on the tops of the trees and watched carefully until the sun changed the limbs high above us from dark silhouettes to bright shades of green, red, and gold. At sunrise the blue jays arrived first to scold us from their lofty perch. They reminded me of one of my teachers at school with blue hair and the same squawking voice. I knew we would only tolerate them for a short time. They would fly away to annoy someone else when the shooting started.

Ours were not the first shots fired that morning. Shots came shortly after daybreak from every direction. In the distance, it sounded like a small war on some far-off battlefield. We waited patiently, eyes still fixed on the treetops and convinced we would catch and pass the other hunters soon. Just a small delay I thought, there will be more squirrels here in a minute than we can legally possess. "Give it time," Dad said. After more time than my patience wanted to allow, we had still not heard the familiar sounds of leaves rustling in the growing morning sunshine. We heard shots though and lots of them coming from my rivals in this unspoken contest. A slight north breeze that warned that fall would soon give way to winter was the only movement, and Dad sat patiently with a contented smile. My impatience soon gave way to dread as the morning wore on. What if we did not go in with the limit? Forget being there first. I had heard enough shots to know that we would not be the winners in today's competition. Now I was concerned we may not even get a shot. What was I going to say to those other boys I had bragged so much to last night? Maybe when we walked back past the river, there would be a boat. I could paddle to the Mississippi then down to New Orleans. In New Orleans, I could catch a boat for Australia. Dad had said that Australia was the land of opportunity and maybe no one there would have heard about my failure on this: the worst opening day

"Just Common Sense"

of my young life.

We stayed in the woods longer that morning than had ever been necessary. The shots in the distance had stopped long before we got up to leave, picking up our empty hunting coats that grew too warm for comfort as the morning wore on. Dad still had that silly smile he had worn all morning, and not only did I not understand it, it made me mad. Frustrated and discouraged, I walked along side Dad back to what, I was sure, was going to be an embarrassing reunion with the others. As we walked along the river, there was not a boat to be seen anywhere.

There was excitement and laughing when we finally arrived at the cabin.

"How many ya'll got?" were the first words I heard.

"We had a tough morning," Dad replied. "We thought they'd be there for sure, but it turns out they were where you guys hunted, it looks like."

Everyone had a successful hunt that day except for Dad and me. Everyone had the limit, and no one could believe we did not even get the first shot, especially me. The grown-ups got busy getting lunch ready while the boys lined up all the squirrels on the front porch and bragged about how great their hunt had been that morning. What happened to us was a question that I got tired of trying to ignore.

As the men cooked over the open campfire and the boys made gestures as if they were shooting up into the trees, I found an opportunity to escape to the river alone. Dad saw me slip away down the trail that led to the rope we had tied to a branch in a Tupelo tree beside the river. On hot summer days, we boys would swing out on the rope over the river and let go to drop laughing into the cool, muddy water. Those were happier days. Dad followed as I made my way to the riverside, I guess, because I looked like I just might hang myself on that rope.

"Tough day, wasn't it?" Dad asked.

"Yea," was all I could manage.

"It was a good day though. We spent the night and the day with good friends," he went on.

Good friends, I thought. I was mad at all of them and would probably never speak to any of them again. I just looked up and down the river for that darn boat.

"Good friends, good food, and an opportunity to do something we love. What more could anyone ask for?" Dad said.

"I'll tell you what we could ask for; we could ask for getting our limit. We could ask for just getting a few. We didn't even fire our guns!" I shouted. "We didn't even see one," I moaned.

"No, we didn't," Dad said softly. but we did see a lot of good things.

We saw our friends have a successful day. We saw fathers and sons spend time together with each other. We saw boys turning into men, and we saw men get a chance to act like boys. It was a good day, and Lord willing, we will get the chance to do it all over again tomorrow. I want you to realize, son, that today's failures are not fatal. I want you to cling to the hope that tomorrow will be better. No need to be discouraged. As long as there is tomorrow, we get another chance for success. It's just common sense," Dad assured.

Chances did come through the years, and Dad and I spent countless hours chasing squirrels and sitting beside rivers looking for boats to come and take us away to lands of opportunity. Some hunts were successful and some were not, but they were all memorable. I learned to not be so consumed with the outcome and learned more to enjoy the opportunity.

"Just Common Sense"

Getting the limit is important to 13-year-old boys. Teaching me that holding on to hope and not to become discouraged was important to men like Dad; it was just common sense.

Chapter Six

MALICIOUS MISCHIEF

"...it's wise to watch others and learn from theirs as well."

Malicious mischief was the official legal term assigned to rock throwing when I was fourteen years old. Dad had told me to look the judge in the eyes, and I was trying hard to do what I had been told — at least this time. The anger in Judge Lowell's eyes made them spin like one of the rides at the fair that made me want to lose my corned dog when I rode it. Of all the windows in all the broken down old shacks in my hometown, I had to pick his to use for target practice. I knew I was in trouble this time and looking him in the eye was not going to get me out of it.

The trouble actually started when we lied to our parents about camping out that night. We were camping out all right, but we were really using that as an excuse to stay up all night and wander the streets. Momma had told me to be in the sleeping bag by midnight because if I were up after 12:00 a.m., I was probably up to no good. As usual, Momma was correct with her prediction. It was about 2 o'clock in the morning when the police walked right up behind us unnoticed and slapped us in irons. We thought we were getting away with our crime since the lights never came on in the big house. Now I was headed to the big house with all the other hardened criminals, except I had to call my parents. My friend's mom and dad came right away to bail him out; mine allowed me to spend the night to make sure I learned my

"Just Common Sense"

lesson. Dad had been a "hell raiser" in his youth and knew I had earned the experience I was about to receive.

My cell was four paces from one end to the other and two paces from front to back, yet they found room to put the commode right in it. I must have walked fourteen miles that night back and forth like a caged lion trying not to come in contact with that commode. I hoped that whatever they fed prisoners did not have bran in it. I did not have a mattress or covers, just a metal slab hanging from the wall with holes in it. All I could think was what were the holes for. There was no way I was going to lie down on that excuse for a bed and even if I did…what were the holes for? I had no window to the outside world, and the door slammed shut with an echo that sent chills through my bones. I did not even have a harmonica or a metal cup to rub across the bars. It was the longest night of my life, and Dad knew it would be.

The sun was rising when I heard footsteps coming down the concrete hallway. I begged the desk sergeant not to open the cell, but with a grin on his face, he did it anyway. Without a word, I followed Dad down the corridor to freedom and disaster, I thought. I got in the car with my head down and rode with it in that same position thinking if he takes a swing at me, the blow would not hurt as bad on the top of my head as much as it would in the mouth. I had always been accused of being hard headed, and this time maybe it would pay off. I rode in silence as we headed down and familiar road, but it was not the road that led home to the safety of my Momma. I was sure she would have a hearty breakfast for her little convict and would want me to wash off whatever I had been walking in all night. I recognized the house immediately; I had been to Mr. Dole's house with Dad many times in the past. What were we doing here now, I thought? Mr. Dole owned a construction company and surely, Dad was not going to discuss building plans in the frame of mind I had put him in. Dad got out and disappeared into the house. Several minutes later Dad and Mr. Dole emerged from inside, and with grim looks and puffed out chests, they made their way to my side of the car. I knew there was a great possibility that I was either going to throw up or find myself sitting in a puddle. I had not used the rest room all night; no way I was using the one in that cell. When Dad opened the door I knew I had better stand at attention, control my bladder, and swallow whatever was trying to come up in my throat. Dad always said, "Sometimes you got to be like a jackass in a hail storm; just turn your back to it and take it." That's what I was preparing to do.

"Apparently, Dad said, "since school is out for the summer, you have found yourself with too much time on your hands. Bobby here is going to help you with that. You will meet him at the end of our driveway at 7:00 a.m. You will do whatever he tells you to until he brings you home at 5:00 p.m. Do you understand?"

I understood from hearing Dad talk about Mr. Dole that working construction was hot, tiring, dirty work, and I understood this wasn't going to be any fun, and I also understood there was something about child labor laws.

"Yes," was all I could get out at the time. I also understood it would have been a mistake to mention the other things I understood at that point.

"I doubt you'll feel much like staying out all night and throwing rocks when Bobby here gets through with you," Dad said. Those words held a profound truth I could not have fully understood at that moment, but I came to understand very soon.

I worked six days a week from 7 till 5 with a 30-minute lunch break. I built scaffolds, carried brick and mortar, picked up debris from around job sites, and did every bad job that no one else wanted to do for the entire summer. I had never

"Just Common Sense"

wanted, no, needed, school to start back so badly in my life. It was hot, tiring, and dirty just as I had thought, and why anyone wanted to do it was more than I could grasp. I figured the other laborers must be out of jail on work release just like me, and that is why they were doing it. I did learn to chew tobacco. It was great until the juice found it is way down my throat, and I had to spend most of the day lying on a pile of bricks in the shade. Mr. Dole docked my pay but did not tell Dad. I was grateful to him for that. I also learned some cool new vocabulary words that summer. They would eventually get me in trouble again later, but I used them freely on the job along with all the other guys. The one thing I learned most is a tremendous respect for those who build and work with their hands. I did not want to do it for the rest of my life, but I was glad they did, and I learned to admire their craft and work ethic.

That summer seemed like an eternity as I mashed fingers, toes, and banged my head into everything from cement mixers to mortarboards. Having that hard head came in handy more than once that summer except for the footing I dug in the wrong place. Mr. Dole made me do it over again with a square ended shovel. It was something to do with learning my right from my left, and I would probably need to know that at some point in my future. As Dad had predicted, I did not feel much like going out at night and certainly had no desire to stay up until 2:00 a.m., even on Saturday nights.

Finally, the summer mercifully came to an end, and so did my torture, I thought. It turns out I was a good laborer, and Mr. Dole and Dad figured out a way for me to work on weekends and after school. This lesson was never going to end, I thought. I was going to have to pay with sweat and blood for the rest of my life for one silly mistake. The only thing that saved me was football. Dad loved football; and if I wanted to play, he would support me. I thanked Mr. Dole for the painful, agonizing; dreadful opportunity to work in the blazing hot sun for little or no pay; my debt to society had been paid.

I never knew how much Dad had to pay for those windows. The money that I made working for Mr. Dole was never asked for, and I did not have enough sense to offer it until it was too late. Dad installed the windows on his day off, I discovered some years later. Dad had also been on the police force for a short time, and he knew all the guys that were there the night I was brought in. How that must have embarrassed him. I also found out many years later that Dad had sat in the waiting room all night during my incarceration just to make sure I was going to be okay. I did not have to suffer learning my lesson alone; he was right there with me and he suffered as well. Dad mentioned that night to me only once for the rest of his life. He said, "Son, learn from your mistakes, and it's wise to watch others and learn from theirs as well. Remember what you learned and don't repeat the mistakes. It's just common sense."

I have spent years memorizing quotes from famous people. I like what Socrates wrote: "Employ your time studying other men's writings so that you may come more easily by what they had to work hard for." I'm sure Dad never read Socrates, but in his own fashion, he knew that learning from others whether it was knowledge of what to do or what not to do was just common sense.

Chapter Seven

GOOD MISS

"...I could not be prouder, it was a good miss."

Only during hunting seasons would Dad and I ever a miss a weekend Turkey shoot. These were social events on the grandest scale. Folks would drive from as far away as Paducah, Kentucky, which was a three-hour drive if you drove the speed limit and may have well been the end of the earth. If it were not, a 15-year-old boy was sure he could see it from there. Food was spread out on folding tables for all the spectators and competitors to enjoy. There was everything from sliced tomatoes, right out of the garden, to homemade cakes and pies made from old family recipes with secret ingredients. Knife swapping, storytelling, and lying would give these events a carnival-like atmosphere, but the main reason they were so well attended was the shooting.

A turkey shoot got its name from the prize, not from the actual shootings at turkeys. Shooters would take turns shooting at and hopefully breaking clay targets called skeet or birds, and the best shot of the day would win a huge turkey or ham. Hams were the most coveted prize and not those city hams either, but country hams that were cured in salt and hung in the smokehouses until ripe perfection. Those were the hams that made the best red-eye gravy and 30 minutes after eating, you had to drink a gallon of water or sweet tea to dehydrate yourself. Calling them ham shoots just never sounded right, I guess, and so turkey shoots were what Dad and I lived for in the fall of 1969.

There were usually five stations or five marks on the ground, each a little further back from the previous one where the participants fired. Five birds were thrown from a mechanical thrower, usually a short distance in front of and to the side of the first station. A couple of guys would hunker down behind a propped-up hood of an old car, load the birds on the thrower's mechanical arm, and yank the string that sent the birds flying across a clay dirt ravine when the shooter yelled, "Pull." If all five birds were broken at the first station, then the shooter stepped back to the second station, and the whole thing started over. As long as they continued to break targets, they kept moving back all the way to station number five, and anyone breaking all 25 birds had won the appreciation and approval of the crowd. Contestants continued competing until one by one they were eliminated, and the person breaking the most targets was declared the winner. Often in a day, it would take four or five rounds before the winner could be established, and that was what Dad called, "some really fine shootin."

By the time I was 15 years old; I had been shooting in the contests for three years and had the good fortune to win my share of turkeys and hams. The "old timers" praised Dad for raising a boy with "the eye" for pointing a shotgun, and he especially enjoyed it when I "smoked" the targets. Smoking the target was accomplished by hitting the clay bird dead center with the shot, and it would disintegrate into a puff of smoke in mid-air. That would really get the crowd going, and you knew that your aim was true. At other times the targets, if not missed altogether, would break into noticeable pieces, which meant the target was hit and counted but not dead center. It was a near miss.

My nickname in 1969 was "dead-eye Dan" by the regulars at these events because it had been my year for

"Just Common Sense"

winning most them. Dad's expression seldom changed, but I knew how proud he was by the nods of approval he gave me before I received the prize. He really liked ham, and I was happy to be able to earn my groceries for a change.

A grand final shoot had been scheduled before the weather got too cold to stand outside. Wearing too many clothes made shooting difficult, and duck season was fast approaching, so by November a $1,000.00 first prize had been donated by some local businesses for the last shoot of the year. That was more money than I knew existed, and it made the 20-mile drive from home even more frustrating. Folks from three states would attend, and some of the best shots from those states would participate. Dad drove, and I fidgeted for what seemed like hours.

I made it through the first set of shooters with relative ease, but as the afternoon wore on, the competition got stiffer. I was shooting my Remington 870 that Dad had traded my old single shot 410 gauge and $30.00 for three years earlier. I had shot rabbits, squirrels, and ducks with that old gun, as well as thousands of cans and bottles on the many trips Dad and I had taken together. When I made it to the second round of competition, I was shooting against guys that had real skeet guns. They were purchased with winnings from events bigger than this one and had never even been fired at anything except clay targets. I looked out-classed in my blue jeans, tennis shoes, and flannel shirt, especially shooting that old gun, but luck was on my side. I thought my luck had run out when I sized up my opponent in the final round of the day.

He had on shooting glasses with the yellow lenses that made things look brighter and clearer and one of those fancy shirts with the shoulder patch sewed right on. He had a leather shooting vest that held his shells and another pocket for the empty hulls. Guys like him reloaded their own shells with those hot loads of extra shot and powder. Guys like me bought them off the shelf when they went on sale. He looked like he had stepped out of the pages of <u>Field and Stream</u> magazine, and I looked like a 15-year-old kid with an old shotgun that had no business being there. Dad's nod is the only thing that kept me from running to the car and hiding.

I hardly remember making it through the five stations. It seemed that the old 870 shotgun was pointing itself and that it was someone else that yelled Pull in that crisp fall afternoon. I had made it all the way through without a miss. Most of the targets had been smoked, and the crowd let me know that I was the favorite in this competition. I was the underdog, and now it was the big dog's turn. I wish I could say that I was being a good sport and cheering for my competition, but that would be a lie, I wanted him to miss. I was rooting, if only in my mind, for him to fail. I wanted to win and more importantly, I wanted it to be his fault and lose. Dad stood beside me and cheered at each bird that he broke. All I could think is what is going on here; did he want this thing to go to sudden death?

That is exactly where we ended up. We had each gone through all five stations without a miss, and now the competition would be head to head. Each shooter would fire at one bird each, taking turns until someone missed, and this time smoking the bird was the object of the game. Breaking off small pieces, a near miss would not be good enough at this point. Only dead center hits would impress the judges. We flipped a coin to see who would go first and I won. Dad had always said he preferred to go second in these circumstances because then he knew what he had to do. It was difficult to stand there beside this guy and let him have the first shot, but I thought Dad knew best in these matters. We were at the fifth station, all the way back; the best shot would win.

"Pull!" he yelled, and the bird flew straight across the ravine.

"Just Common Sense"

"Smoke!" yelled the crowd; and though I was not watching, I knew the outcome.

It was my turn and as I readied myself, this guy in his fancy clothes with his fancy gun and his special reloaded shells, bent over and said, "Good luck." I think he really meant it, and I watched him move back to give me

more room. I barely remember hollering, "Pull." The only thing I will never forget is that gust of wind that caught the target about 35 yards out. The clay bird rose ever so slightly as it rode the wind just out of the pattern of my shot, and a small piece broke off one side. It all seemed like slow motion and though I had hit the target, it was not going to be good enough.

Dad made me congratulate the guy for his victory and shake his hand. He said the guy had not taken me seriously at first, but something about me being a good competitor and how proud he was to beat me. Beat me was the only part I understood. Dad and I drove home in silence and the 20 mile trip home seemed even longer that the trip getting there.

"I'm sorry," I managed to get out before we pulled into our driveway.

"Sorry for what, son?" Dad asked.

"I'm sorry I missed," I replied.

Dad stopped the car under one of the pine trees we had planted when we first moved into our new home. We sat there for several minutes when Dad finally said, "Son, you have nothing to be sorry for. You gave a great effort. Through ability, practice, and determination, you went all the way to the finals. When other folks may have counted you out, you did not give up on yourself and you did you best. There could be only one winner of the prize today, but I think everyone knows there was more than one winner there. I could not be prouder and you should be too. It was a good miss."

I missed hitting the target dead center, but not the whole target, Dad went on to explain. He talked about those that did not get in the competition and those that sat on the side only to watch. I realized as the evening wore on that it's those that do not make the effort to hit the target that do not get the chance to win. I had put myself in the middle of the competition and had come up just a little short, but in his common sense, Dad pointed out that it was good miss.

Chapter Eight

TRAFFIC

"...It's okay and I'm right here with you."

In an era of peace marches, hippies, and going to San Francisco with flowers in your hair, driving, I was convinced, would be my key to happiness in 1970. Well, it was not really the driving; I had been doing that for most of my life, and it was the freedom everyone spoke about in 1970 that I thought driving would provide for me.

I was very small when Dad would hold me in his lap and allow me to steer his car on fishing and hunting trips. Driving boats was a natural part of my growing up, and I had learned to drive every tractor on my uncle's farm by the time I was ten years old. We always lived where Dad, "could go outside naked if I want to and not see any neighbors," so we always had a big yard. Big yards required big lawnmowers, and I mastered staying out of Momma's flower beds and the new pine trees Dad and I sat out when we moved into, "the last house I'm ever going to build," Dad said.

When I was 14, Dad saw fit for me to learn to work. Mr. Dole, the construction company boss, saw fit for me to learn to drive forklifts, loaders, and dump trucks of every size and variety. In order for me to, "stay out of trouble," Dad would say, he would give me the keys to the old pickup and a fishing boat and tell me to stay at the river all weekend. At age fifteen no kid I knew would argue with that logic. It really was not the driving part that interested me; I got plenty of that. It was the license part and the being legal part and mostly the being grown-up part.

Dad and I struggled often in our relationship, and 1970 was our worst year. I had started to high school in 1970 and had my first real girlfriend in 1970. My music was too loud and my hair was too long for Dad in 1970. My friends and my grades did not make Dad happy either. Looking the way I did, hanging out with the people I was, and making the grades I made were not going to get me in law school, which was always his dream for me. I wanted to spend time without Dad in 1970, with my room door locked, my clothes on the floor, and my bed unmade. My mouth, which kept me in trouble for most of my life, ran uncontrolled in 1970. Dad and I got into a big fight at the dinner table one night; and while we screamed at each other, my momma cried, and I ended up telling him that I hated him. I walked out of the house convinced I would never be able to go back again. It was 1970; I wanted my freedom, and I wanted my driver's license so that I could find it. Momma convinced me to come home and told me that Dad only wanted what was best for me. "If you'll listen," she said, "your dad has more common sense than anyone I know, and he won't keep it to himself, but he'll share it with you because he loves you."

For the rest of 1970, my mouth continued to work overtime, and my ears stopped working altogether. Dad's common sense was eluding me, or the facts are; I was eluding it.

I was sixteen in June, and I had no choice other than to allow Dad to take me to get my driver's license. I had passed the written part, and the eye exam was no problem. Now I had to go take the actual driving test at the highway patrol station on the outskirt of town. I knew from the first minute I saw "Officer Unfriendly," (not his real name), that we were

"Just Common Sense"

not going to get along very well. He was tall, overweight, and did not appear to be enjoying himself, so no one else would either. Someone had actually given this guy a gun, which rode up right under his armpits and the "Smokey the Bear" hat that gave them their nickname in CB lingo was forced over a head that was bigger than the covering. His face let me know immediately that he wanted me to fail and only if I were perfect would I have a chance of passing this last hurdle in the quest for my freedom. The worst part of the ordeal was that Dad, the self- proclaimed best driver in the world, would be sitting in the back seat watching my every move.

The highway patrol office in my hometown is located rock-throwing distance from Interstate 40, and I knew that "Officer Grumpy," (not his real name), would want me to tackle interstate driving. In order to get on the interstate, we had to travel through an intersection that is definitely the busiest in my hometown and maybe the busiest in the world.

We loaded up in Dad's brand new Cadillac. It still smelled the way it did when he drove it home from the dealership, and it would keep that smell until he traded it for a new one. He loved his Cadillacs, and he loved them new. I was still trying to figure out why we had come in his car and not Momma's green LTD when we piled in for the test. I slid easily into the driver's seat, since Dad had it all the way back to accommodate his much longer legs. Dad got in the back seat directly behind me, and the officer finally managed to wedge himself between the seat and the dashboard on the passenger side. I went through the mental checklist the driver study guide recommended and made sure to adjust the seat, steering wheel, and mirrors and, most importantly, fasten the seat belt, which was growing in popularity in those days. With the car started and pointed to the north to take us out of the drive and onto the highway that led to freedom, I froze. Traffic was darting and dodging on the four lanes that lead north and south and the east and west lanes were filled with drivers that glared at me as the officer in the car with me was doing at that very minute. I could literally feel his eyes burning into the side of my face.

"It's clear," he said. "Take off and get on the interstate heading west."

We sat motionless.

"It's time to go," he declared.

My foot remained firmly planted on the brake pedal.

"I've got other tests to give, so you can go anytime now," he finally demanded.

I was trying; I really was, but there was nothing happening except my focus on all the traffic that sped by before me. I was gazing at so many cars and trucks, and so many thoughts kept running through my mind, the least of which was that I was failing this test. My hands gripped the steering wheel as if I were trying to choke it, and my leg hurt from the pressure I was putting on the brake pedal. This all took place in seconds, but it felt like an eternity.

Driving was not a problem for me; I had been doing that for years. I could drive anything I could sit in, sit on, or be strapped to. The problem in those agonizing seconds was the traffic. I had never driven in traffic before, and I was paralyzed by the thought if it. All the driving I had done in the past was in cotton fields, on dirt roads and construction sites, boat trails, and off the beaten path. The most cars or trucks I ever saw were on the gravel road that led to the skinny-dipping spot at the river we boys hoped would be used by the models we saw in our Dad's magazines. It never was, but we kept going there full of hope. Now all my hopes and dreams were vanishing before my very eyes. The battle for freedom was being lost, and I was doomed to being held

"Just Common Sense"

prisoner for the rest of my life.

As he had always done before, Dad came to my rescue. No matter what I had put him through recently and no matter how hurt he must have been by my words and actions, he wanted me to succeed, and he wanted me to overcome my fear. I could feel his breath on the back of my neck as he said, "Son, you have to pull out in the traffic now. This is no different from all those times before, except for a few more obstacles you will have to deal with, and you have what it takes to handle them. Take your time and draw on your experience. It is okay and I am right here with you. I know you can do it."

With his words I lifted my foot from the brake and pulled into the traffic that moments before had held me captive. I had needed a gentle nudge of confidence; and regardless of the obstacles or the fear I had of failing, I remembered dad always said, " If you have a wall in front of you that you can't go around, go over or dig under…just bust through it."

We all have walls that are either real or we just make them up. Those walls keep us captive and keep us from realizing our dreams. I wanted freedom in 1970, and I thought my driver's license would help me get it. Regardless of our problems, my Dad wanted to help me find it too, and his encouragement and common sense did. No decent parent wants to send his kid out into traffic, but Dad knew that was the only place I would find my dreams. Dad also knew that in order to bust through walls sometimes we need a shove.

Chapter Nine
THE MAN
"...it's his money, he's the man."

August in West Tennessee can be a grueling and agonizing month with temperatures hitting the high 90's and humidity that will almost equal that. The heat index can be what Dad called, "damned unbearable." It was the "dog days" as the old timers called them. That means your dog will bury himself in a hole he dug under the front porch and not even come out to chase the neighbor's cat or a biscuit, and now that's hot. It was in these shirt drenching, heat-rash-causing dog days of August that in 1971 the cruel taskmasters we called football coaches held two-a-day practices. That means if they don't kill you running, blocking, and tackling in the hot mugginess of morning, they bring you back in the afternoon when it really gets bad and try again. Twice daily in the punishing heat we practiced the game that would cause the fans to yell and the girls to giggle at in the fall. Football was an opportunity for some of us to go to college, and it was an opportunity for all of us to learn words like teamwork and pride. I was dedicated and passionate about football at age 17, and my Dad could not have been prouder if I were the mayor, a job, which he said, I could do better than the incumbent could.

Dad missed the morning practices because of work, so I rode my bicycle the five miles one way each morning at 7:00 a.m. It was a 10 speed, but it was still hot; and though

"Just Common Sense"

Dad never missed an afternoon practice, I had to ride it back home in the evening because Dad was not going to put it in the trunk of his Cadillac and risk possibly scratching his paint. In the height of the heat during those afternoon practices, I could hear Dad yelling encouragement from the sidelines. He never coached; he would "leave that to the professionals," he said, but you could hear my name being used with lots of flowery expletives in the afternoon heat.

Dad had been quite a player, his buddies had often told me. However, going to school and playing had been cut short by his father's death when he was still very young. His strong back was needed by his brothers to support the family, so he gladly delivered newspapers by horse and buggy and picked up odd jobs when he could. It was at this time that Dad discovered his talent for shooting pool. He worked with his brother running a local pool hall and found time between cleaning and racking balls for a penny to practice the game he told me never to take up. By the time Dad was in his teens, he was making "good money" for those days. Hustling pool, going back to school, and playing football were not a priority, so giving me the chance to do it became his passion. He loved watching me play and never missed my games or practices whenever possible.

I had worked on weekends since I was 14 years old; and during the first part of that summer before practice began, I had managed to save $500.00, and that was enough Dad said, "for a good used car." A car of my

very own. That sounded too good to be true. I had walked all over the county, ridden my bicycle over three counties and hitch-hiked most of West Tennessee by the time I was 17, and now the thought of my own car was almost too much for me to take. I could run head first into other guys in the blistering heat of two-a-day football practices, but my own car made me weak-kneed at the thought. No more borrowing

Momma's green LTD to go on dates with my little red-haired girlfriend, no more walking to her house and then hoping her mom would feel sorry for me and take me home, no more hitch-hiking which Momma hated, and no more bicycle, which I hated. Dad said it was time for us to go car shopping, and he would pick me up after practice to find my own set of wheels. If we found one, I would have to stop and put my bicycle in my trunk because Dad was not concerned about my paint.

I was hot, tired, and still trying to dry off from my shower when Dad

and I headed south on Highway 45 to one of his friend's used car lot. Dad said that Bud had "dependable" cars and integrity: two things that Dad looked for when making any purchase. I was not concerned with the man's character and was sure I did not want "dependable" either. My dog Pete was dependable, and my old 870 shotgun was dependable, and I loved them both dearly, but what I wanted in a car was "sexy." I wanted a car that was sleek and fast with lots of chrome. I wanted loud mufflers and big slick tires like the guys who drove the Cameros and 442's. I wanted to be seen and heard coming; and if it were a stick shift, I would have died and gone to heaven right then. There is a "big" but coming, and here it is; my Dad and my pocketbook said instead of sexy you need dependable. By the time we had driven the three or four miles to Bud's Used Car Lot, I gave up on the sexy and figured my dog, gun, and my red-haired girlfriend would not care as long as my new car was dependable.

When we arrived, Bud came running as if he were shot out of a gun. He was smiling and talking fast before we actually got out of the car and acted as if we were the only customers he had seen for days. Bud knew that when Dad showed up it was not to kick tires; he was there to buy

"Just Common Sense"

something and we were getting the full treatment. Dad had purchased several cars from Bud through the years; and though Dad drove a new Cadillac only, he trusted Bud enough to buy for my momma and other family members that sometimes found themselves in a pinch. Bud was often one of Dad's fishing partners, and he knew he had a live one on the line with Dad. I stood with my hands in my pockets surveying the lot for a Chevelle or Malibu sport and barely heard Dad when he asked Bud if he remembered, "my son."

"Good to see you again, boy," Bud managed to get in to his sale pitch.

I was sure that he really was not, but I did not care. The next thing Dad said Bud and I both heard through his insistent talking and my impatient searching because it shocked us both.

"Bud," Dad said, "my son is here to buy a car. I'm going inside and wait in the air conditioning. We both stood there stunned, neither of us knowing what to say or do next.

"Charlie," Bud yelled, "what did you have in mind?"

"Don't care," Dad yelled back. "It's his money. He's the man."

It was several seconds before we both composed ourselves enough to start our search. Over the next two hours, I drove almost every car on the lot, negotiated the best I had learned from going with Dad on many of these adventures before and listening to enough stories about one owner cars to last me for a while. Dad had always told me that the seller always has two prices: his asking price and his taking price. Dad had always also said that the buyer has two prices as well. His giving price and the "Oh, my gosh, I can't believe he agreed to take that; let's get out of here before he changes his mind" price. The last one was what Bud and I agreed to on— a blue-green, 1964 Chevrolet Impala that had enough trunk room for 10 friends and lawn chairs when we snuck into the drive in theater, as well as my bicycle.

When we made our way into the air-conditioned waiting room, Dad was sitting back drinking a coke and watching television. Bud asked, "Charlie, how you going to pay for this car?"

"I'm not," Dad said. "My son is the man; he worked for his money; it's up to him how he spends it." Then Dad went back to watching his program and left the financial arrangements up to me. I paid cash and told Dad I would meet him at home.

After picking up my bicycle at school, I stopped by my little red-haired girlfriend's house to show off a little and headed home. I took Momma and Dad for a run around the neighborhood before driving to all my friends' houses to let them oh and ah over my purchase. I made sure I let them know that I had made the whole deal without any help and that I was sure that I got a bargain for the money. I was the man!

Dad never asked what I paid for the car, and I do not believe he ever knew. He did tell me later that he was proud of my working hard and earning the money to pay for it. He told me he was proud that I decided to pay cash and not have payments because that was what he would have done as well. My dad was always "the man" in these types of situations, and he had learned to trust his judgments and instincts.

In the hot dog days of August in 1971, he turned over the roll of being "the man" to me, so I could learn to trust mine. That was Dad's common sense approach to life and the living of it. The care and upkeep of my new investment was also given over to me. I never asked Dad to buy a tank of gas. The least I could do for being trusted with man-like decisions was to act like one.

Chapter Ten

FLY FISHING

"...there are two kinds of people in this world."

Dad said, "You need another hobby like you need another hole in your head," when I told him about my new found attraction for fly-fishing. Several friends of mine had gotten into it for its communing with nature appeal, which was popular in the 70's, and I just thought it was the coolest thing I had ever seen. Chasing native trout in their serene environment armed only with sprigs of hair and feathers tied to the smallest hooks attracted me for it's me against nature aurora. I had always been carried away with all the trappings associated with fishing. I liked fishing rods and would spend hours at the sporting goods store picking up each one and shaking it in front of me to test the action of the tip and the firmness of the backbone. I liked fishing lures and managed to collect some priceless gems, well at least to me they were, but I always managed to snag and lose most of them in various water impoundments throughout the southeastern United States. I liked boats, outboard motors, and even minnow buckets. There was not anything that I did not like about fishing, and now the bug for fly-fishing had bitten me. Every cent I could scrape together I would gladly spend to scratch the itch of this new bite. You might say I was a fishing nut, and the fruit did not fall far from the tree in my family.

Dad's nickname growing up in rural West Tennessee near the Tennessee River was "Fish" by his brothers and friends because of his love for it. As a kid he could not afford to buy bait, so catching his own bait occupied his time until he had caught enough worms, lizards, frogs, or whatever he thought a fish might eat, and then he'd head down to the creek, pond ,or river for a day of fishing. My grandmother said that most every evening one of Dad's brothers would be sent to fetch Dad home for dinner, and most of the time he would be found with a stringer full of fish to bring home and clean.

By the time I was eighteen years old, I had spent thousands of hours dragging boats over cotton fields and beaver ponds to those "secret holes" Dad knew about. He even blindfolded me once to keep me from finding my way back with my friends to one of his special places. He said, "I don't want a beaten path down to my best spots," and he figured the best way to keep anyone out was to make sure they could not find their way back— even me. If it were 20 degrees or 100 degrees, you better be prepared to spend the day because going home early was not an option for Dad. Rain did not matter to Dad either. He said, "The fish are wet anyway; if they don't mind, we shouldn't."

No amount of work was considered too much, and no amount of time was dedicated to the pursuit ahead of time. We would stay as long as it took, so there was no need for watches and time schedules. The night before was for packing and gassing up trucks and outboard motors. There were batteries that needed charging, coolers that needed filling with drinks and ice, rods, and reels that needed checking to make sure we had an edge over our competition. We sharpened hooks and tested fishing line for knots or bad spots called frays. Dad wanted every opportunity for success and would not lie down to rest until everything was finished and ready for an early departure. Dad worked hard at fishing and expected anyone who was fortunate to be invited along to work as hard as he did.

"Just Common Sense"

Days on the lake with Dad were long, leisurely outings designed to teach a young boy the value of nature. He was not after the solitude or the pensive thought-provoking silence. He had no primal need to be out of doors; and if you thought he was a man of few words in his normal mode, in his fishing mode, he was a mute. As a kid growing up, our outings were not opportunities to inquire about my plans for the future or what I wanted to be when I grew up. They were not opportunities for him to reminisce about by-gone days and discuss his past successes or failures. By the time I was 18, Dad said he would "leave all that value of nature stuff to me and my long-haired hippie buddies." When Dad sat out to fish, it was serious business, and he was determined to go home with what we could lawfully possess.

By 1972 after all the days I spent with Dad pursuing his passion, I finally figured out Dad's real obsession, and it was not fishing at all. All that junk I had heard about how he patiently would sit for hours and would work so hard to catch his bait and how he always asked landowners permission before using their property was not because he loved to fish. I recalled by age 18 that Dad never really had a very good attitude about all the activity surrounding getting ready for a fishing trip nor did he have a really good attitude about waiting them out. He got no real joy from all the activities he put up with to go fishing or the actual acts of baiting, casting, and waiting; but he got tremendous joy from watching his bobber go under and feeling the tug against the drag of his reel. Suddenly when a fish was on Dad, he was 10 years old again, and it was more fun to watch him reel one in than to catch one yourself. I have never seen anyone who loved battling a big one more than my dad. It was not fishing at all that Dad loved so much; it was catching. He put up with the getting ready part, he put up with noisy kids in the boat, he put up with the heat or the cold, and he put up with all the other activities, so he could enjoy and bask in the satisfaction of the result... catching fish.

It was a beautiful Friday afternoon in late April 1972, when I told Dad about my new passion for the pursuit of trophy trout, armed only with split bamboo rod, drag less reel, and 2 pound tippet on the end of my floating snag less fly line. I thought he would pass out from laughing.

"Where are you going to find trout around here?" was his first assault on my new hobby. You going to bug school, so you can learn to match the hatch," he scoffed, using terminology reserved for only fly fishing purists such as myself. His last blow before leaving for the Western Auto store to get something he needed for our trip tomorrow was, "Don't let the neighbors see you standing in the yard with a newspaper under your arm practicing your casting technique; they'll laugh us out of the neighborhood."

I was furious; I had spent several of my hard-earned dollars slaving at Mr. Dole's construction company on all this stuff, and the least Dad could do was be supportive, I thought. I knew we didn't have trout in the muddy rivers and lakes around home, but I was determined to learn this new fishing technique, and I had read about guys traveling the world fly fishing in the <u>Field and Stream</u> magazines I received each month. I will show him, I thought; I will catch a world record, and then he will not think it was such a waste of money. I will do something he never has done, and he will be sorry he laughed at me when I get my picture in one of those magazines.

I spent the rest of the evening in my room planning how I would show my Dad how wrong he was, how right I was, and how he was not the only one who was a good fisherman. I was mad, and I was mad enough to let Dad go alone tomorrow on what would be a beautiful Saturday in the spring in Tennessee. The dogwood trees would bloom soon, and the crappie would surely be biting, but Dad would have to go without me. I would show him; I might never go with him again if he were going to have that attitude.

When Dad arrived home from the Western Auto store, he was still chuckling under his breath as he hollered for me to come out of my room and help him with hooking up the boat and getting ready for our trip tomorrow. I told him I was not going and went back into my room without any further explanation. "Have it your way," I heard him call out as I was closing my door and retreating into my solitude to continue my pity party.

By the time I awoke Saturday morning, I was sure that Dad would be

on the lake and be catching fish as fast as he could bait up. 7:00 a.m. was well past the time Dad normally would leave because he always wanted to be on the water at daylight. "Ready to go when the fish wake up," he would always say. I walked slowly to the kitchen only to find him sitting at the kitchen table drinking strong black coffee, which was the way he liked it.

"It's late; why are you still here?" I asked.

"Waiting on you," he replied.

"I told you I wasn't going," I said.

"I know you did, but I thought I'd wait on you anyway," Dad said.

"You made me mad yesterday," I vented. "I spent a bunch of money on that stuff, and I think I'd enjoy giving it a try. You know you do not know everything. I was hoping we could try it together sometime. I was thinking we might make a trip to Arkansas over Christmas because that is supposed to be the best time for big trout. The least you could have done was be a little more supportive."

I could not believe I was saying all those things. When they came out, they sounded worse than when I had said them in my head the night before. Dad asked me to sit down and if I wanted a cup of coffee.

"Son," he began, "there are two kinds of people in this world. There are activity-oriented people and there are results-oriented people. I know exactly which one I am. I only care about the results and only put up with all the activity because I know it has to be done in order to be successful. Fly-fishing looks to me like a lot of activity for very little results, so I know it does not fit the kind of person I am. I made a mistake yesterday when I made fun of you. You may be an activity type, and I did not consider that. I looked at it only from my point of view. That is a mistake because it takes all types, and we need to understand which type we are and which type others are because that is the only way we get along and get things done. We need each other, and we need to work together. Let's go fishing."

Dad and I did go fishing that day and many other times through the years. We even made the trip to Arkansas at least two times each year — in the spring and the fall, until his health would not allow him to go any longer. Dad would use his old bait casting equipment and catch about five times as many fish as I would with my fly fishing outfit, but he never mentioned it. He was after the result, but I was fishing for something else. I was fishing for his approval, and I was fishing for his strength of character. I was fishing for more time to spend with him and to learn the common sense he taught about knowing who you are and knowing others and learning to accept our differences, so that we can work together effectively. Dad would say, "If we don't learn to work with each other, neither one of us will have any fish to eat."

Chapter Eleven
THE SPARE TIRE
"...strive for the very best customer satisfaction you can provide."

I believe the last thing a 19-year-old young man wants to do is take his dad car shopping. At least it was the last thing I wanted to do, especially with my dad. Someone else may have written the book about <u>The Art of the Deal</u>, but Dad perfected it many years before. Dad always traded for his new Cadillac on Saturday before the new models rolled out. "That's when you get the best deal," Dad would say. "The dealer needs to get the old models off the floor to make room for the new ones." Saturday was magic to Dad as well because the dealer would be busiest on Saturday and would therefore be the most vulnerable. "He'll need to get us out of there," Dad would say, "because he's got so many prospects and only so many hours in the day." However, it was never quick, and Dad did not want it to be quick. It was an artful dance that he and the same guy went through every year at this time, and I did not want to watch. I was leaving for college at the end of the summer. I had to report for football practice soon, and I needed to be training. If I would win a spot on the team, I'd have to be in peak form, and I needed to start packing and there were friends to say goodbye to, and this was not how I wanted to spend my Saturday watching these two go at it. However, Dad needed me. He had a cast from above his knee to his foot from a broken leg he had suffered with for months. He needed me, and I needed to be there for him even if I knew I was going to hate every minute of it.

The dance began with Dad hobbling around the lot on his crutches looking at every Cadillac sticker and reading them line-by-line. His rival peered out from the windows of the office feeling no pity for Dad in his injured state. I believe he thought Dad probably was just trying to use the cast for sympathy, and though he admired the effort, sympathy was not going to help Dad get a better deal. Dad and Mr. Evans had been playing this game for as long as I could remember, and I think they both just really enjoyed it. Mr. Evans would wait before coming out of the office until Dad had looked at every car on the lot. They would go back inside and dicker on the one Dad had decided on for hours. Dad would get up to leave at least two or three times; Mr. Evans would follow him yelling something about his kids' shoes and how he wasn't in business to give cars away. After they had each argued enough and threatened to never do business with each other ever again, they would shake hands, and a deal would be done. Dad would pay cash, Mr. Evans would be able to buy shoes for his kids, and the dance would be over until the same time next year. This was not how I wanted to spend my Saturday, and I could not imagine anyone else really would want to either.

I made myself comfortable in the waiting room with others that were getting service or were waiting for their new car to get the final clean up before they took them home. I had not eaten my way through the first bag of popcorn when Dad appeared in the doorway and said, "Let's go." Let us go where, I thought. Surely, this was not over this quickly. I didn't want to be there, but since I was, at least let's get our money's worth of the free popcorn, and there was a <u>Field and Stream</u> magazine I hadn't had a chance to look at yet.

"Where are we going?" I asked.

"Just Common Sense"

"Just get in and let's go," Dad said.

Okay, I thought, this is a new tactic. Dad had brought me for some other reason than to drive; now I get it. He was using me to get a better deal somehow. I drove slowly to the exit looking between Dad and the rear-view mirror. Mr. Evans would run out soon and stop us, I thought, or Dad would tell me to turn around, but it did not happen. We exited from the parking lot and headed toward home. The most convenient way home from the car dealership was to head east on Interstate 40 for a short distance. Dad told me to get on the interstate but to head west instead.

"That won't get us home," I said.

"I know where home is," replied Dad.

What had happened was all I could think about as we drove the 80 miles to Memphis that morning. Dad directed me to the Cadillac dealership and within 30 minutes, we were riding in a brand-new gold Cadillac Coup de Ville heading toward the interstate, then east bound and home. When

Dad finally started talking, again he was like a kid in a candy store that had eaten too much sugar. He was playing with all the knobs and trying out all the buttons on his new prize. He loved his Cadillacs, but mostly I think he loved being able to keep his promise to himself of owning one. It was a promise made as a young kid growing up poor. He liked the color, the leather interior, and mostly the wood grain dashboard. "Makes it look rich," he said.

I was still in shock of what had happened with Mr. Evans earlier and how quickly the deal had been put together in Memphis. When Dad finally calmed down, I asked him to tell me what had happened.

"Well, I told the guy in Memphis what I wanted and

how much I wanted to pay; he agreed, and here we are."

Wait a minute, I thought. Dad had been buying cars from Mr. Evans for years, and they played hundreds of games of give and take. They had both enjoyed the battles, and both had enjoyed the victories. What happened this time? Why did Dad buy a car from... a stranger? I needed more than he just agreed to my price; where is the satisfaction from that? They did not even argue or raise their voices or spend the whole day horse-trading.

"Give me more than that," I said to Dad.

"He agreed to give me an extra spare tire," was Dad's reply.

"What? A spare tire?" I heard myself ask.

"Yea," Dad said. "Here I am spending more for a car than the first house I ever owned, and Bill wouldn't throw in an extra spare. If you have a flat and need your spare tire, then you don't have a spare. Makes perfect sense to me that you don't want your customer sitting on the side of the road broken down when all it would have taken was a little extra effort to satisfy the customer. The guy in Memphis threw in an extra spare."

I shook my head for the rest of the drive home. My dad had done business with a complete stranger in a foreign town and not even enjoyed the victory that comes from battle with a worthy opponent over a spare tire. I asked Dad to explain to me later as he watched me pack to go away to college why the spare tire was such a big deal.

He said, "Son, you are leaving to begin your college career; then one you'll work in business yourself. The most important thing to any business is their customer. Sometimes the customers make unrealistic requests, but how you handle their requests will help determine your success. Always strive

"Just Common Sense"

for the very best customer satisfaction you can provide; it's good common sense."

Dad never purchased another Cadillac from our hometown dealership. He found a new rival in a different town that enjoyed his style of horse trading and strived for common sense customer satisfaction. How much does a spare tire cost? Sometimes it costs you a customer.

Danny Williams

"Just Common Sense"

Main Street Publishing, Inc.
206 E. Main Street Suite 207
P.O. Box 696
Jackson, Tn 38301

Toll Free #: 866-457-7379
or
Local #: 731-427-7379

Visit us on the web:
www.mainstreetpublishing.com
www.mspbooks.com

E-Mail: mspsupport@charterinternet.com